NOT FAR FROM THE JUNGLE

OTHER BOOKS BY ABNER DEAN

It's A Long Way To Heaven
What Am I Doing Here?
And On The Eighth Day
Come As You Are
Cave Drawings For The Future
Wake Me When It's Over

Cleveland  New York

THE WORLD PUBLISHING COMPANY

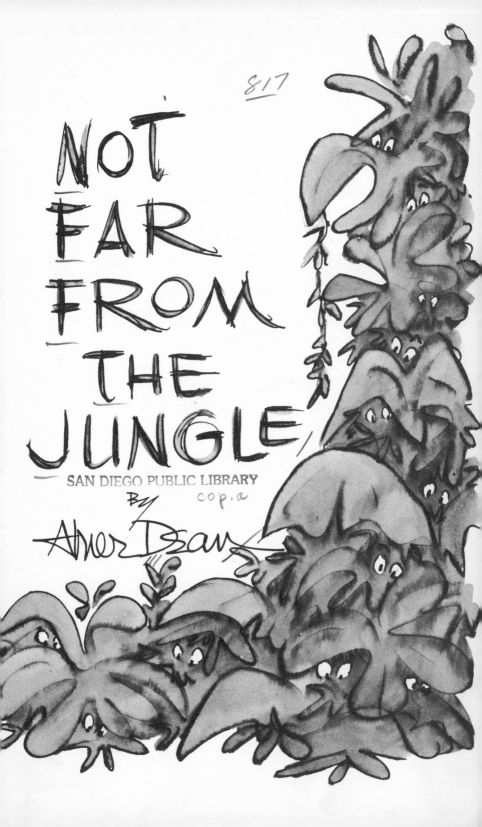

NOT
FAR
FROM
THE
JUNGLE

BY

Abner Dean

Library of Congress catalog card number: 56-7824

First Edition

AH856

To the involuntary expatriates of the
Central Park Zoo in Manhattan, where
I began to write this . . .

CONTENTS

FRAGMENT FOR A LANDING PARTY 9

IN WHICH TEARS FALL IN THE BRIMSTONE 11

SLEEP BEFORE MIDNIGHT 13

GENTLE WORDS TO A FRIEND 15

YOU CAN'T GET THERE FROM HERE 17

NEVER REPROACH A ROACH 19

WIDE AWAKE MUTTERINGS 21

SLIGHTLY TARDY THOUGHT 23

RHYME TO BE TAKEN BETWEEN PILLS 25

SEX 27

LINES TO BE RECITED WHILE NIBBLING A BUNCH OF SOUR GRAPES 29

LLINES 31

HORIZONTAL OBSERVATION 33

AND SO TO BED 35

RHYME WHILE STARING AT A SILENT PHONE 37

WATCH OUT FOR THE GIRL NEXT-DOOR 39

INSIDE DARKEST MADISON AVENUE 41

ONE FOR THE SUGGESTION BOX 43

WHAT A WONDERFUL RUT! 45

LOWER MATHEMATICS 47

LINES ON BECOMING THE OLDEST MAN IN THE WORLD 49

WISHFUL LOVING 53

LET'S DRINK TO SOMETHING 55

SHORT THOUGHT 57

WITH AN EAR COCKED FOR THE SECOND KNOCK 59

AMOR CANIS 61

IT CARRIES YOU BACK – DON'T IT? 63

TO BE HUMMED WHILE SITTING OUT ON A GREEN LIMB 65

WARNING FOR AN AMATEUR AMORIST 67

COTE NOTE 69

RECAPITULATION 71

LINES WRITTEN ON THE BACK OF AN OLD I.O.U. 73

L'APRÈS-MIDI D'UN CARTOONIST 75

THE RHODE ISLAND REDS ARE ORGANIZING 77

WHAT A NIGHT FOR BAYING AT THE MOON 79

THOUGHTS IN A GROWLING BASS 81

ROUND AND ROUNDELAY 85

LINES FOR A TATTOO 87

PRELUDE TO SILENCE 89

ALTRUISM 91

A BEEF ABOUT BEARS 93

SONG FOR A DAY-OFF 95

WORDS TO BE SPOKEN AT THE FIRST SIGN OF AN ULCER 97

HALLUCINATION 99

BETTER NEVER THAN LATE 103

THIS IS GOOD-BYE, I HOPE 105

RHYME FOR A RESEARCH FOUNDATION 107

LINES WRITTEN IN A ROOM WITHOUT A VIEW 109

NONSENSE FRAGMENT FOR A SONG 111

I'M GLAD I'M NOT A SNAIL, HEY! 113

CARESS BEFORE CURFEW 115

HAIL TO THEE, BLITHE SPIRIT 119

VERY LATE AFTERNOON THOUGHT 121

FRAGMENT FOR A LANDING PARTY

Not far from the jungle
I sat down
And cried
When I measured
The distance
We covered
Outside —
And I saw
The whole crew
Of us
Puffed out
Like sails
Because
One or two
Of us
Sloughed off
Their tails.

IN WHICH TEARS FALL IN THE BRIMSTONE

I had a chat with Satan
And Satan was feeling low.
"Look what they've done to sex,"
Said he,
"They're ruining my show!"

"Since time began
I worked for man —
I gave the best years, man and lad.
I tried to show the universe
The primrose path from bad to worse—
But now they can't tell good from bad
Since surveys made each former vice
Seem normal, healthy—even nice."

"I think", cried Satan,
"I've been had!"

"What'll they think of next?,"
He cried —
And as he cried he shook —
    For all I know he's crying yet —
    I left to have a look.

SLEEP BEFORE MIDNIGHT

Be off to the analyst's hay,
My love –
Tell him about your dream.
I don't care what you say,
My love —
Now that you're off your beam.
I don't care where you lay,
My love —
Any old couch will do.
All that I want to say,
My love —
Is
Shoo, my love –
Please shoo!

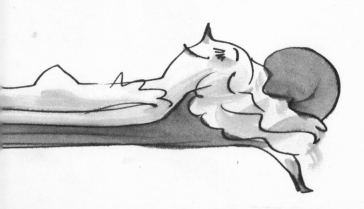

GENTLE WORDS TO A FRIEND

You're a brave little guy
Looking truth in the eye.
I'm impressed
By the things that you see.
But why do I find
That your truth is inclined
To uncover
Some error in me?

I don't
For a moment
Dispute that it's true —
But, do me a favor
And keep it to you . . . ?

YOU CAN'T GET THERE FROM HERE

They told me money wasn't all
When I was very young—
That there was love
And wine
And songs
Awaiting to be sung.
And so I started singing
And they told me to shut up—
And that's when first I learned
That only money fills your cup.

Money makes your voice sound sweet-
Money makes your cliche's wise—
Money buys top-round to eat—
Makes her sigh the sigh of sighs.
Money makes your phone to ring—
Money it's that bells the cat—
Money is a funny thing
But more important than all that
It makes the whole world for you itch-
Remember
Money makes you rich!

NEVER REPROACH A ROACH

Roaches are smart.
Roaches are brighter than you think.
Centuries of thought they've had
Without a missing link.

Go and read your Genesis —
You'll find writ down
These menaces
Were here
Before was Adam,
Madam.

So
If you're sneaking up on one
Be sure of your approach.
Just don't pit your wits
Against the wits
Wots in a roach.

WIDE AWAKE MUTTERINGS

Listen, Fate,
Up to this date
I, silent stood
And caught each fast one,
But the straw you tossed me now's
The last one.
So, just to ease the pain of it
Let me, Fate, explain a bit.

An ancient saying has it
That a wife,
To be perfection,
Should
In the salon — be polite,
In boudoir — a confection,
And in the kitchen, making chowder,
An economist — cum lauda.
But
The last one
That you sent me
Really takes the cup —
She's politest in the pantry —
In the salon — off her head,
And just to get it all mixed-up
An economist in bed.
(I hope you'll do better next time.)

SLIGHTLY TARDY THOUGHT

If we hadn't
Had a few —
You'd have had
A better view
Of me —
And I of you.

RHYME TO BE TAKEN BETWEEN PILLS

The thing about female careerists
That's worst
Is
They won't be content
Till the roles are reversed.
They've girded their loins
And they've only begun —
And they'll never give up
Till the job has been done —
Till male becomes female
And female is male —
And only a wiseman
Will know head from tail.

And analysts all over town
Have grown wealthy
Telling these girls
Their desires are healthy —
So
After the nonsense
These analysts fed them
It's funny
That none
Of the analysts
Wed them.

SEX

Something given
For joy in the pauses
Has been made
The base
Of contractual clauses.

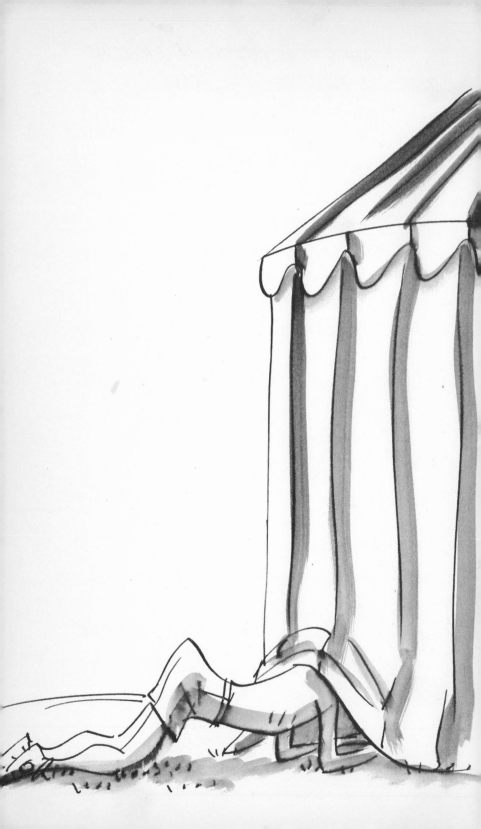

LINES TO BE RECITED WHILE NIBBLING
A BUNCH OF SOUR GRAPES

I've almost been there —
Where V.I.P.s
Cushion their tails
On the lush settees
Of golden women
Employed to please
Megalomaniac V.I.P.s.

I almost, but never,
Got the keys
To enchanted gardens
Of such as these.

But I came just close enough
To find
The girls weren't golden —
The men weren't kind —
And their public relations people
Lied.
I know
I've been
On the winning side.

LLINES

I saw a llama in a zoo
And just to be polite
I stopped and said,
"So, llama, nu—
How spent by you the night—?
    You're looking somewhat drowsy!"

The llama stood on all his toes—
The llama looked me
Down the nose—
And carefully
One word he chose,
    "Llousy!"

HORIZONTAL OBSERVATION

She's so particular
Perpendicular—
But
Off her axis
She relaxes.

AND SO TO BED

Never
In the plays I see
Does anyone
Resemble me —
Nor have I,
When the whole thing ends,
Seen
Any of my friends.
And as it goes
From set to set,
I never see
Someone I've met —
And yet
Each critic and his wife
Proclaims these plays
Are true to life.

I'm sure the critics know their stuff—
I guess I don't get 'round enough.

RHYME WHILE STARING AT A SILENT PHONE

No one
To play hookey
With —
Be off
And see
A bookie
With —
To dine
On wine
And cookie
With—
To sit
In cran
Or nookie
With
And think
Of rhymes
With "ookie"
With.

WATCH OUT FOR THE GIRL NEXT-DOOR

The day that I met
Angel-face
All the parts
Fell into place —
All the things
I never knew,
Were true.

But one thing
I will never get —
She told me
We already met.
I guess
I wasn't
Ready yet.

INSIDE DARKEST MADISON AVENUE

Oh have you seen
The natives dancing —?
Strutting more than twice their size—
Posing, posturing and prancing
On this avenue of lies?

All day long the mad momentum—
Each day like the other was —
In a tribal trance that sent 'em
Grovelling to Great God Duz.

Oh have you seen
The natives group up
As the sun begins to sink —
And together how they soup up
More than they can hold of drink?

Then the natives
To their houses
Crawl—
Their brains still wrapped in fuzz —
In a coma
Kiss their spouses —
And dream till dawn
Of Great God Duz.

ONE FOR THE SUGGESTION BOX

If you
Can do
Without
It —
Don't boast
About
It !

WHAT A WONDERFUL RUT!

There's lipstick
On my shirts again.
I'm getting over
The hurts again.
Someone's picking
My ties again.
Loving
With open eyes again —
But a voice
Is beginning to say again
It will end
In the same old way again.

LOWER MATHEMATICS

When it comes to finances
She's a whiz —
Deposits in hers —
Withdrawals
From his.

LINES ON BECOMING THE OLDEST MAN IN THE WORLD

What will I say
To reporters today
When they pump me again
For the reasons
I've piled up another four seasons?

Now that I've reached
This incredible age,
(Just by the trick of not dyin')
They pretend that
My silliest statements are sage—
But I know
That they know
I'm lyin'.

I lied
When I told them
The secret was booze,
Which I always pretended
To swim in.
And the year before that
I made scandalous news
By just saying,
"Wimmin, more wimmin!"

And once, for a gag,

I whipped out a bag
Of nutmeg
And started to munch —
And I looked at them straight
And told them,
"Of late I only eat nutmeg for lunch."

At a hundred and two
I told them I knew
That it's work
And more working that did it —
But I lied
And I gladly admit it.
Since the day in my youth —
When I found out the truth —
That work
Is what makes people sick,
I've never done more than a lick.

You get the idea —
(I could go on from here) —
Each year after year
What I'm after
Is achieving a reason that's dafter—
Just to add to the general laughter.

But
Whatever I've quipped

I've stuck to the script —
And,
While tweaking the world
By the nose,
I've never stepped
On any toes.

But today
When reporters knock on my door
To question
My gerontological love —
I'll finally tell them
The truth of my story —
The reason
A few of us only
Grow hoary.
I'll tell them
I never saw anyone old
Who ever blew
Hot —
Who ever blew
Cold.
Don't hate —
Don't love —
Don't take sugar pills —
It's not only hating
But loving
That kills.

WISHFUL LOVING

Just say you love me,
Don't try to tell me why —
Say it
Like an angel
On vacation
From the sky.

Just say you love me.
Don't promise to be true —
Just promise
That you'll love me
Till the day
I say
We're through.

LET'S DRINK TO SOMETHING

As I go from bar
To bars —
I notice how few
Statements parse.

I'm not sure
Should I blame the drink
Or blame it
On the way we think.

SHORT THOUGHT

She's expensive
But not dear.
Why
   don't
      I
        get
          out
           of
             here?

WITH AN EAR COCKED FOR THE SECOND KNOCK

Still looking—
Still hoping someday I'll find
The horse of another color,
The grass of another kind,
The wagon to hitch a star to,
The island to sail afar to,
The sky-pie the poets write of,
The goal that I'm just in sight of,
The ship that's about to show up,
Someone to get the dough up—
Even a split-week booking!
But I'm still
Still looking.

AMOR CANIS

Amo, amas, amat —
What is it that she's got?
She adds up wrong
And all along
I knew
I shoulda not.
But wrong or right
All day and night —
Amo an awful lot.

IT CARRIES YOU BACK—DON'T IT?

Way down
Upon the Old Subconscious,
Far up the creek,
That's where
They fish for
Fancy trauma
Five times a week —
That's where
They float around
On couches,
Going aground —
That's where
The psychiatric ouches
Loudly
Resound.

Way down
Upon the Old Subconscious,
Day after day,
That's where
The odd folks
Pay!

TO BE HUMMED WHILE SITTING
OUT ON A GREEN LIMB

The winter
Has a-went away,
The spring
It has a-come.
The summer
Soon
Will simmer
Down
And kow-tow
To au-
Tumn.

And so the
Panorama goes —
And it will
Never stop —
Nor will
The daily
Hammer blows
I get
My head
On top.

WARNING FOR AN AMATEUR AMORIST

Love is all right,
It's just
Not very bright —
And while I
Don't mean to quibble —
You're not being smart
If you eat out your heart
Or let
Someone else
Have a nibble.

COTE NOTE

I frequently
See pigeons—male—
Follow closely
On the tail
Of pigeons
I assume are shes.
And when the shes
Give hes
The breeze —
It's strange
How
With the greatest ease
The hes
Pursue still other shes—
As though in their particular hay
All pigeons are a dove-like gray.

And, though I never saw one caught,
Assuming that she is, I thought:
   "The mathematics of the chase
   May be the male's way
   To save face."

RECAPITULATION

Red rover, red rover
Let Jennie come over—
Let Jennie come over and play.
It's raining outside
And though I have tried—
I don't feel like working
Today.

Red rover, red rover
Jennie's been over—
Jennie's been over and went.
And I suddenly know
When we played long ago
None of us knew
What it meant.

LINES WRITTEN ON THE BACK OF AN OLD I.O.U.

If I had a dime
For every time
I miss you
When you're away—
We could both settle down
And be broke,
My love,
Just like we are today.

L'APRÈS-MIDI D'UN CARTOONIST

I thought when I kissed
The cross-eyed muse
That life would have only
The rosiest hues—
All to gain
And nothing to lose —
But now,
Alas and alack,
I suddenly
Have for myself
Some news—
There are days
When I'm sorry
I kissed that muse
And the cross-eyed muse
Kissed back.

THE RHODE ISLAND REDS ARE ORGANIZING

While laying eggs
A hen once said,
"Examined I should have
My head —
The price of eggs
Is up, I read,
And
I'm still paid
In chicken feed."

WHAT A NIGHT FOR BAYING AT THE MOON

I wish
I could
Persuade
You to
A place in mind
Without a view —
Just a loft
With nothin' more in
Than a soft
And springy floorin'
And a bucket of Vouvray—
And
You and I adorin'
As we're lost
In lovin' play.

THOUGHTS IN A GROWLING BASS

I hate women
Who flirt with waiters,
Who ring too often
For elevators —
Who wander,
While they dine with you,
To see who else is there
Who'll do —
Who stay in powder room so late
You're not sure that you have a date.
But even so
You know the truth —
They're phoning from an outside booth
Some phoney, just to keep in touch,
Or leave a number
Where they'll be
Just in case some random he
Decides to join the relay race—
And, if you tire,
Take your place.

I hate women
Who lose their bag

Or tell a joke
And lose the tag —
Or leave a glove
And make you fetch—
Or talk like at
A cricket metch—
Who wag their tails
When males are near
And stare
As though you
Weren't here —
Who tell the taxi
Where to go,
Pretending
That you never know—
Who interrupt
Your best bon-mots —
I'd like to
Punch them on the nose.

ROUND AND ROUNDELAY

Wassailing — wassailing —
Downing the sudsy foam
Forgetting there's anything ailing
Forgetting it's time to go home.
Forgetting ever to hit the hay —
Rounding the bend of another day
Like a sailor rounding the Horn.
Wassailing — wassailing —
And glad that we were born
To go
Wassailing . . . (etc. into the night)

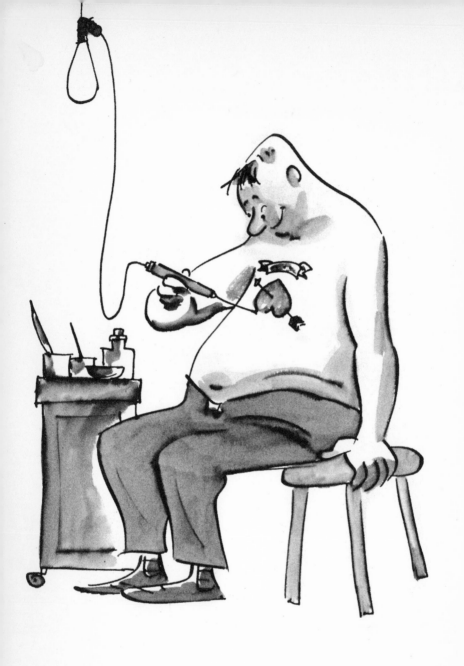

LINES FOR A TATTOO

No one
Knows
About anyone —
Ever.
And
That's what
Makes
Falling in love
So darn
Clever.

Some morning, early —
Right before bomb-drop,
I'll just be sitting here
Nibbling a gum-drop.

My mission has always been
Only to find
Which color gum-drop
Is best of its kind.
And now all my research
Is ending in waste —
There are so many colors
And all the same taste.
And I yet haven't found
In a test
Of them all —
Pound after pound —
Which is best
Of them all.

So I'll just go on testing
And stare at that sky-dot
And ask myself, "Why?"
And I'll also ask, "Why not?
Nibble a gum-drop
Just before bomb-drop?"

ALTRUISM

All
My own
Wild oats
Are sown —
(The pleasantest
Of chores) —
So
If you
Have some
Of your own
I'll gladly
Help
With yours.

A BEEF ABOUT BEARS

I find that bears
Are awful bores —
The way they waddle
On their paws —
The way they get up
From all fours
As though I owed them
Wild applause.
I'd make a law,
If I made laws,
Containing only this one clause —
And I quote:
"No bear can run for office
And it can't even vote."

SONG FOR A DAY-OFF

I feel
Very "is"
To-day —
Real
"Mis-en-scene."
I feel
Very "am"
And
"Will be"
And
"Have been."
I feel
Very
Very
A part of
"To be" —
It's awful
Peculiar
I don't feel
Like "me."

WORDS TO BE SPOKEN AT THE FIRST SIGN OF AN ULCER

Now's safari
Type of weather—
Let's pack up
And trek together—
Leave the world
Of vows and pledges
And return to
Jungle edges.
You leave him
And
I'll leave her—
And
We'll start out
As we were,
Just a double blur.

HALLUCINATION (while thinking that art is not as longa nor life as breve as the art critics make them.)

I saw
Van Gogh and Gauguin
Sitting in a hogan
Drinking
Their lives away.
Sitting at sun-up
Working a bun up.
Here's what
I heard them say:
"Have one more
Sloe gin",
Said Van Gogh
To Gaugin.
"No, Gogh",
Said Gaugine,
"I drink
Chateau wine —
Chateau wine is all
That I drink,
Except ink".
"Pardonnez-
Moi didn't think",
Said Vinc.
"But, man

To man, Gogh",
Said Gauguin to Van Gogh,
"Where did our plan go?
It went down the sink.
We vowed
That we'd empty
The rest of the jug."
"Ah, oui",
And
"Ah, ugh",
Said Van Gugh.

Oh
Van Gogh and Gauguin
Sitting in a hogan
Painting
The red-skins red —
They knew that
They oughta
Give up fire-water
And,
Just as they faded,
They said,
"We
Shoulda stood
In our four-post-impressionist
Bed."

BETTER NEVER THAN LATE

Fate forgot
To wind his clock
Reminding him
It's time to knock.
So here I am,
A locked-in mortal,
Staring at
An un-knocked portal.

THIS IS GOOD-BYE, I HOPE

She would have kissed me,
So she said —
She would have led the way to bed—
She may have
If the stars were right—
She might have
On another night.
She talks a past pluperfect bliss—
The present positive's what I miss.
What kind of mixed-up grammar's this?
I'll take a girl who makes some sense
And kisses in the present tense.

RHYME FOR A RESEARCH FOUNDATION

What I'd like to know
About seals
Is what they all do
Between meals.
I know
What they do
When it's lunch
In the zoo
And their bark
Fills the park
With its hullaballoo—
And the guard
Pitches fishes
Right in their face—
Which they all find delicious
Without saying grace.
But when the pail's empty
They dive down below—
And that's what I'm
Wanting to know—
My question:
Do they spend
ALL their time
In digestion?

When I read of hunters
On the veldt —
I never wonder
How it felt.
Or men
Who climb
A mountainside
And blame it on
The mountain's pride —
Or seamen
Sailing on the deep in
Boats just big enough to sleep in—
All of them just leave me
Cold,
But comfortable
As I grow old.
Whatever they are proving by it
Is proof enough —
I don't deny it —
Nor will I ever long to try it.

I'd rather be here
In my chair
Than there
            or there
                  or there.

NONSENSE FRAGMENT FOR A SONG

A little girl's
Kisses
Are very nice —
But
A big girl's
Are Champagne
On ice.
Two little girls
Aren't
Half so good
As one
Big girl
Who is
In the mood.

I'M GLAD I'M NOT A SNAIL, HEY!

Snails live such secluded lives—
Never husbands
Never wives.
Never room
For more than one.
How can snails
Have any fun?

CARESS BEFORE CURFEW

I dreamed you
To a lash
At twenty-three.
Where were you
When the time was right for me?

I knew that
Where you were
Delight would be.
Where were you
When the time was right for me?

A generation now has passed
And here you are
At longest last —
And I,
At forty-three or more,
Now find you
Eager at my door —
Far younger
Than I thought you'd be.
Where were you
When the time was right for me?

Just think —

When you've a hundred years—
Five score—
I'll be a hundred years
Plus twenty-four!

Oh careless girl—
You temporized with fate
And let yourself
Be born too late.

   (But women
   Have a right
   To be
   A little late
   It seems to me.)

HAIL TO THEE, BLITHE SPIRIT

When a whale
I see
Go under—
Being me
I often wonder
How it feels
To be a whale
And kiss
Upon
So vast
A scale.

VERY LATE AFTERNOON THOUGHT

The sunset gun's
About to boom.
The sound of it
Will fill my room.
The wave of it
Will rock my chair,
Concussioning
What's cushioned there —
But
What is there
Will not be me —
I will have left there
Quietly
On exit cue
With cartoon done —
And you can sit and watch the fun.
I will have gone
Before the gun.